BUTTERFLIES

RYAN JAMES

NORWOOD HOUSE PRESS

Library of Congress Cataloging-in-Publication Data

Names: James, Ryan.
Title: Butterflies / Ryan James.
Description: Buffalo, NY : Norwood House Press, 2025. | Series: Insects in my backyard | Includes glossary and index.
Identifiers: ISBN 9781684502448 (pbk.) | ISBN 9781684502455 (library bound) | ISBN 9781684502462 (ebook)
Subjects: LCSH: Butterflies--Juvenile literature.
Classification: LCC QL544.2 J359 2025 | DDC 595.78/9--dc23

Published in 2025 by
Norwood House Press
2544 Clinton Street
Buffalo, NY 14224

Copyright © 2025 Norwood House Press
Designer: Ocean Books
Editor: Kim Thompson

Photo credits: Cover, p. 1 Mrs. Minard/Shutterstock.com; p. 5 muhammadayaz_4/Shutterstock.com; p. 6 ARIES_Studio/Shutterstock.com; p. 7 Ondrej Prosicky/Shutterstock.com; p. 10 Khairil Azhar Junos/Shutterstock.com; p. 11 Stephen Farhall/Shutterstock.com; p. 12 SanderMeertinsPhotography/Shutterstock.com; p. 13 KPIACHKO OLESKI/Shutterstock.com; p. 14 Nadeszhda Bolotina/Shutterstock.com; p. 15 Nejron Photo/Shutterstock.com; p. 17 Baolin/Shutterstock.com; p. 18 Nancy J. Ondra/Shutterstock.com; p. 19 Butterfly Hunter/Shutterstock.com; p. 21 Elnur/Shutterstock.com

Printed in the United States of America

Some of the images in this book illustrate individuals who are models. The depictions do not imply actual situations or events.

CPSIA compliance information: Batch #CW25NHP: For further information contact Norwood House Press at 1-800-237-9932.

TABLE OF CONTENTS

WHAT IS A BUTTERFLY?

Butterflies are colorful **insects** you might see in your backyard. They like to fly around flowers.

BODY PARTS

Butterflies have **antennae** that help them smell and find flowers. A long, coiled tongue helps them drink **nectar** from flowers.

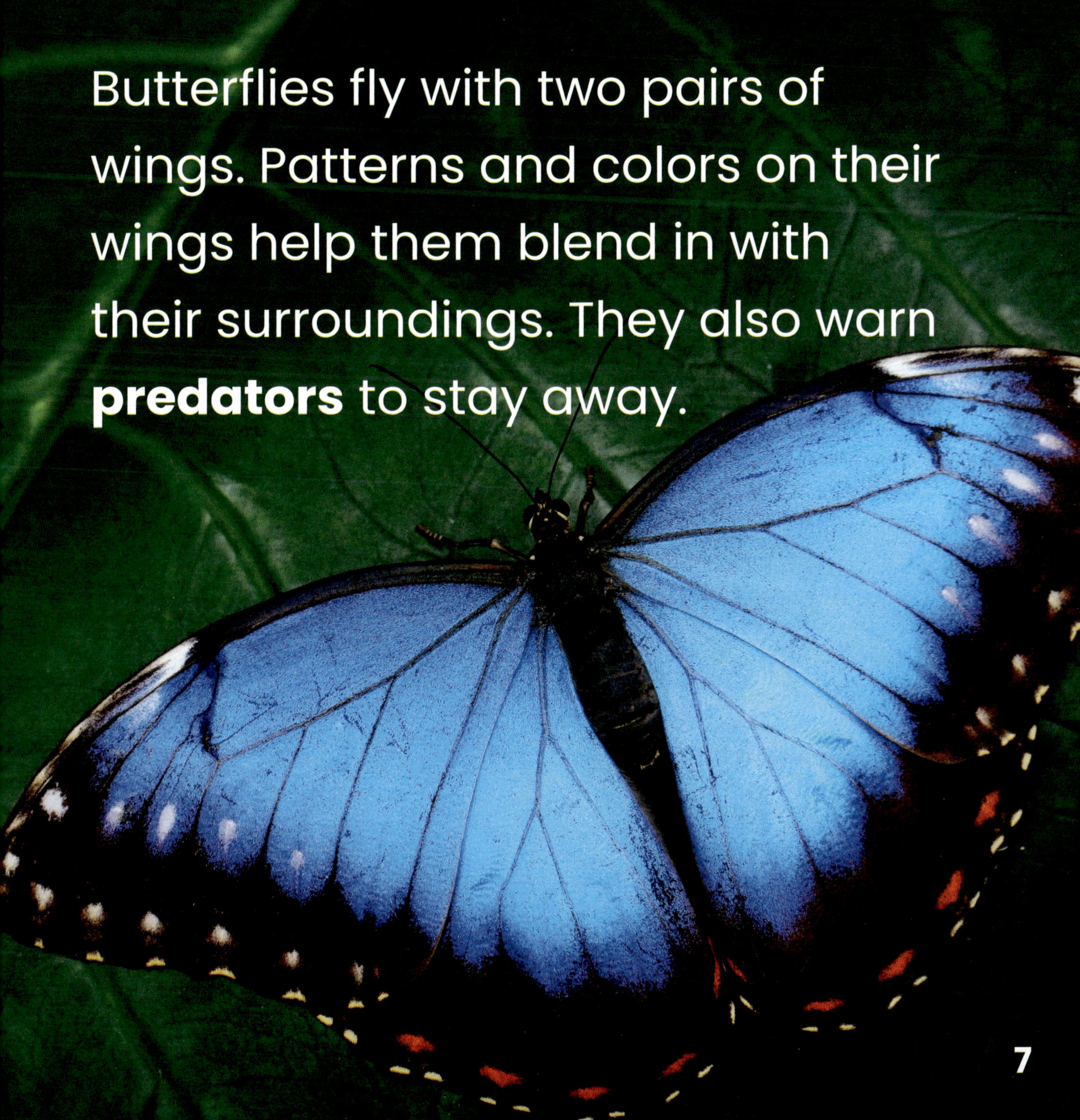

Butterflies fly with two pairs of wings. Patterns and colors on their wings help them blend in with their surroundings. They also warn **predators** to stay away.

The back part of a butterfly's body is the abdomen. It contains the stomach and helps with breathing and **digestion**.

TYPES OF BUTTERFLIES

The monarch butterfly is known for its orange and black wings. It **migrates** long distances, flying thousands of miles each year.

Swallowtail butterflies have bright colors. The tails on their wings look like a swallow's tail. They can be found in gardens and parks.

The painted lady butterfly has orange, black, and white patterns on its wings. It is one of the most common butterflies in the world.

The blue morpho butterfly has bright blue, shiny wings. It lives in the rainforests of Central America and South America.

BUTTERFLY BEHAVIOR

As they drink nectar, butterflies move from flower to flower. They help plants grow by spreading **pollen** from one plant to another.

Butterflies open their wings to warm up in the sun. This helps them fly and stay active.

Butterflies lay eggs on leaves. The eggs hatch into caterpillars that eat leaves and grow. When a butterfly is changing from a caterpillar into an adult, it is called a **chrysalis**.

WHY ARE BUTTERFLIES IMPORTANT?

When butterflies spread pollen from flower to flower, it is called pollination. Many plants cannot make seeds and fruit without pollination.

Butterflies are food for other animals like birds and spiders. They are an important part of the food chain.

Butterflies are sensitive to changes in nature. Scientists can study them to find out if the environment is healthy.

GLOSSARY

antennae (an-TEN-ee): slender, movable, segmented organs on the heads of insects that are used to sense the environment; feelers

chrysalis (KRIS-uh-lis): a butterfly in a quiet stage of development between a caterpillar and an adult when it is wrapped inside a hard outer shell

digestion (dye-JES-chuhn): the process of breaking down food so that the body can use it

insects (IN-sekts): small animals that have hard outer skeletons instead of backbones and that have three pairs of legs, one or two pairs of wings, and three body sections

migrates (MYE-grates): moves from one area to another, especially at certain times of the year or to find food or other resources

nectar (NEK-tur): a sweet liquid produced by flowers

pollen (PAH-luhn): fine yellow powder that is produced in the male parts of flowering plants and that must be spread to female plant parts in order for some plants to reproduce

predators (PRED-uh-turz): animals that live by hunting other animals for food

THINKING QUESTIONS

1. Name three body parts of a butterfly.

2. How are a monarch and a swallowtail alike and different?

3. How do butterflies get nectar from flowers?

4. Why do scientists study butterflies?

5. Why are butterflies important?

INDEX

ABOUT THE AUTHOR

Ryan James lives in the western part of North Carolina with his rescue dog Bailey. As a child, he would search for creepy crawlies as he hiked through the forest near his house. When he's not on the hiking or biking trail, he is cheering on his favorite baseball and football teams.